LED ZEPPELIN

EASY GUITAR ANTHOLOGY

Produced by
Alfred Music
P.O. Box 10003
Van Nuys, CA 91410-0003
alfred.com

ISBN-10: 0-7390-6068-6
ISBN-13: 978-0-7390-6068-1

Cover photo: © Robert M. Knight

Contents

BABE I'M GONNA LEAVE YOU

Words and Music by
ANNE BREDON, JIMMY PAGE
and ROBERT PLANT

Moderately bright, with a half-time feel ♩ = 134

Babe I'm Gonna Leave You - 7 - 1

⊕ *Coda*
Bridge:
w/Rhy. Fig. 2, *cont. simile (see meas. 49)*

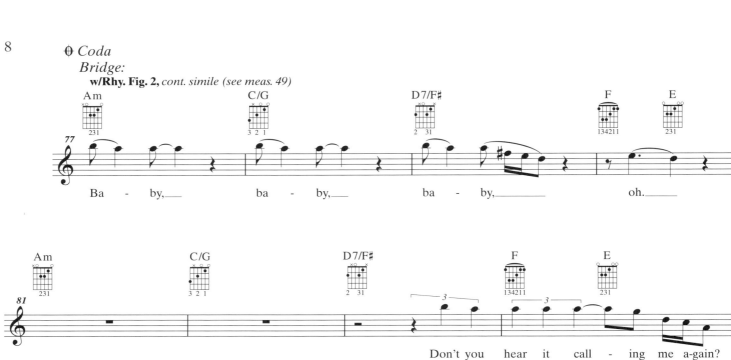

Ba - by,___ ba - by,___ ba - by,___ oh.___

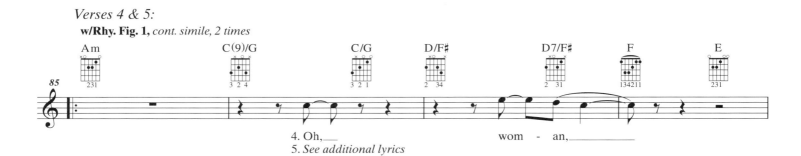

Don't you hear it call - ing me a-gain?

Verses 4 & 5:
w/Rhy. Fig. 1, *cont. simile, 2 times*

4. Oh,___ wom - an,___
5. *See additional lyrics*

wom - an,___ I know,___ I know___ it feels

good to have you back a - gain and I know that one day, ba - by,___ it's real - ly gon-na

grow.___ Yes, it is.___ We gon-na go walk-ing___through the park_ ev-'ry day.

Bridge:
w/Rhy. Fig. 2, *cont. simile (see meas. 49)*

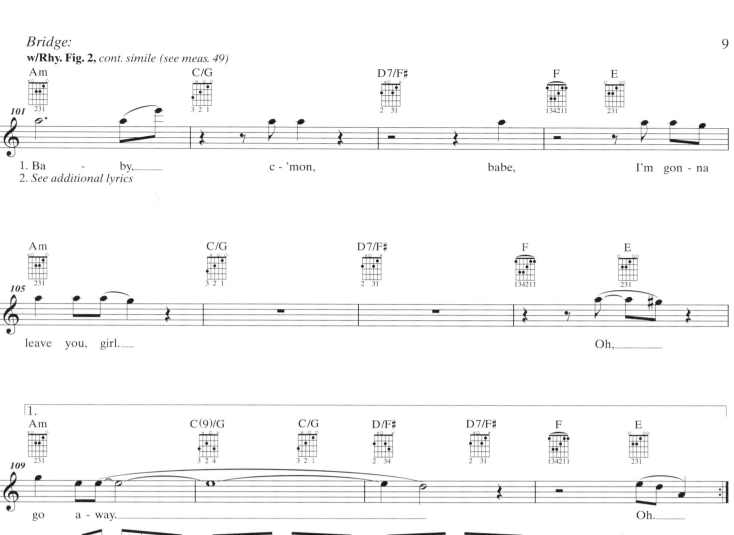

1. Ba - by,_____ c - 'mon, babe, I'm gon - na
2. *See additional lyrics*

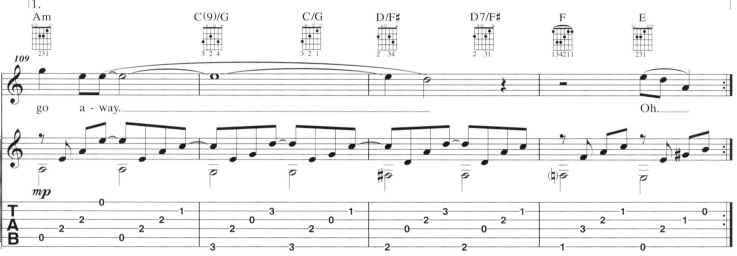

leave you, girl.___ Oh,_____

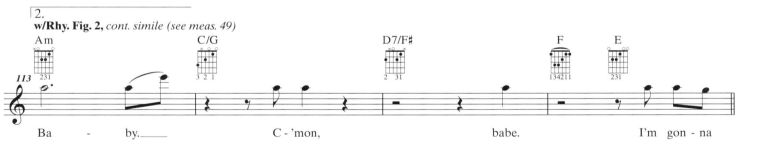

go a - way._____ Oh.___

2.
w/Rhy. Fig. 2, *cont. simile (see meas. 49)*

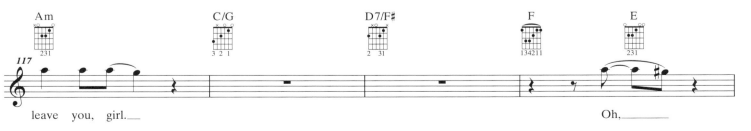

Ba - by._____ C - 'mon, babe. I'm gon - na

leave you, girl.___ Oh,_____

Babe I'm Gonna Leave You - 7 - 6

Outro:
Freely

*Unison E notes played on 1st and 2nd strings.

rit.

*Optional: For easier fingering, high A notes
may be played one octave lower
on the 7th fret of the 4th string.*

that's when it's call - ing me._____ I said that's when it's call - ing__ me_____ back__ home._____

Verse 2:
Babe, babe, babe, babe, babe, babe, baby,
Mmm, baby, I wanna leave you,
I ain't joking, woman, I've got to ramble.
I can hear it calling me the way it used to do.
I can hear it calling me back home.
(To Bridge:)

Verse 3:
I know, I know, I know I'm never, never, never, never,
Never gonna leave you, babe.
But I got to go away from this place.
I got to quit you, yeah.
Oh, baby, baby, baby, baby.
(To Bridge:)

Verse 5:
Oh, miss your lips, sweet baby.
It was really, really good.
You made me happy ev'ry single day.
But now I've got to go away.
Baby, baby, baby, baby.
(To Outro:)

COMMUNICATION BREAKDOWN

Words and Music by
JIMMY PAGE, JOHN PAUL JONES
and JOHN BONHAM

Chorus:

w/Rhy. Fig. 2 *(Elec. Gtr. 2) cont. simile*

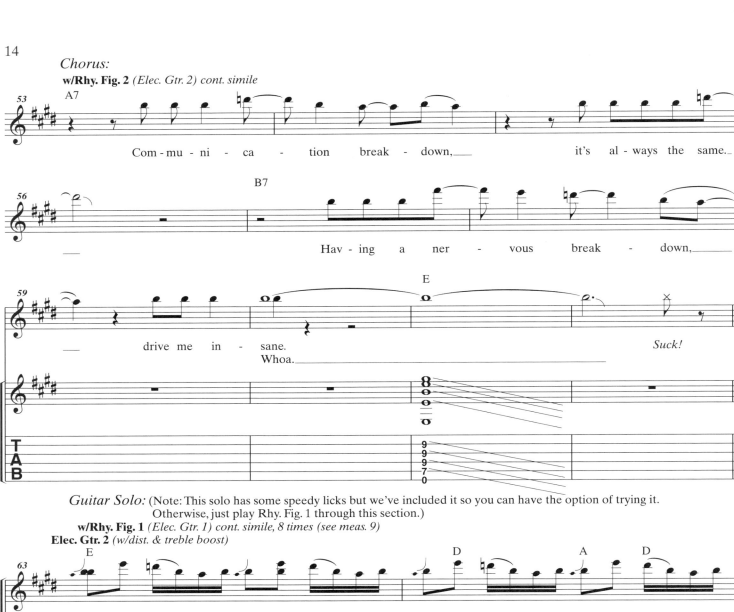

Com - mu - ni - ca - tion break - down,___ it's al - ways the same.___

___ Hav - ing a ner - vous break - down,___

___ drive me in - sane. *Suck!*

Whoa.___

Guitar Solo: (Note: This solo has some speedy licks but we've included it so you can have the option of trying it. Otherwise, just play Rhy. Fig. 1 through this section.)

w/Rhy. Fig. 1 *(Elec. Gtr. 1) cont. simile, 8 times (see meas. 9)*

Elec. Gtr. 2 *(w/dist. & treble boost)*

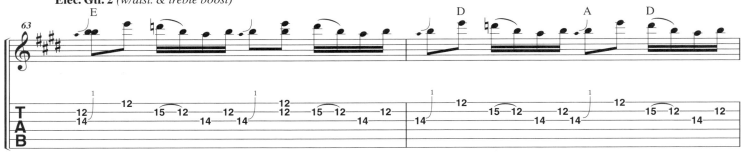

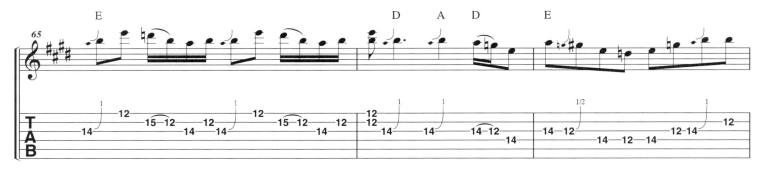

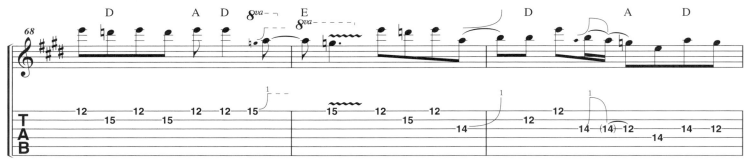

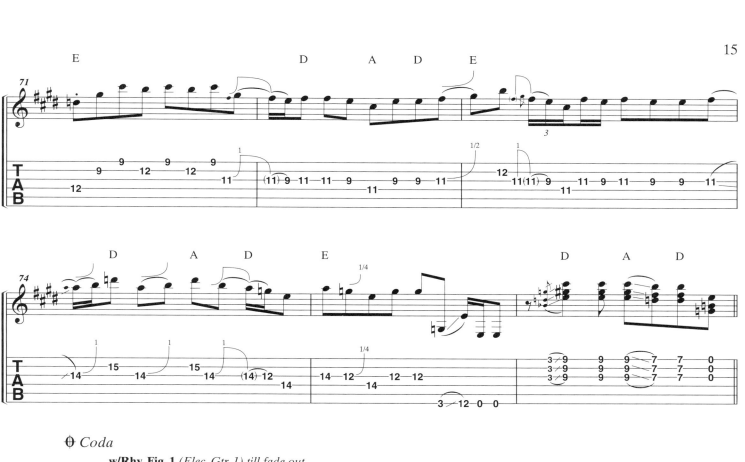

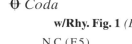 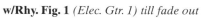

⊕ Coda

w/Rhy. Fig. 1 *(Elec. Gtr. 1) till fade out*

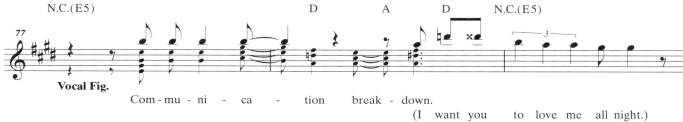

Vocal Fig.

Com - mu - ni - ca - tion break - down.

(I want you to love me all night.)

end Vocal Fig.

(I want___ you to___ love me.___) (Whoa,___

ah, a whoa,___ oh.___) (I want you to love me.)

Fade out

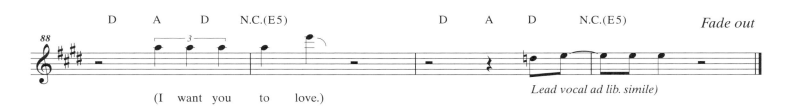

(I want you to love.)

Lead vocal ad lib. simile)

BLACK DOG

Bright ♩ = 168

Verses 1 & 3:

Words and Music by
JIMMY PAGE, ROBERT PLANT
and JOHN PAUL JONES

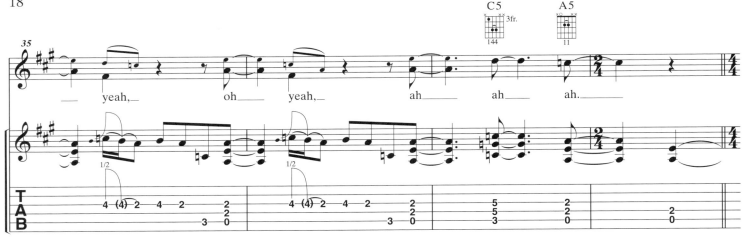

Verses 2 & 4:

2. I got to roll, can't stand still,__ got a flam-ing heart,__ can't

4. *See additional lyrics*

get my fill.__

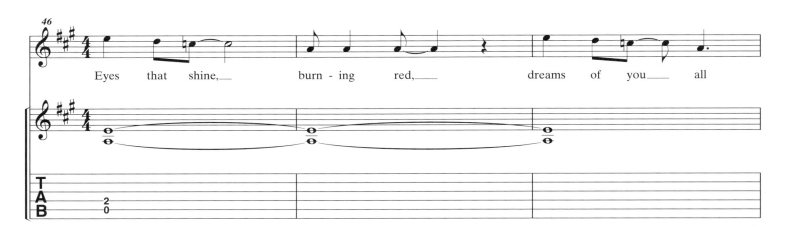

Eyes that shine,__ burn-ing red,__ dreams of you__ all

*Note: Some of the licks in this solo are challenging for "easy" guitar but, if you start slowly and gradually increase the tempo, it's a great introduction to combining major and minor pentatonic scales in a solo.

Elec. Gtr. 2 ad lib. solo (use previous 4 meas. as a model for improv.)

Repeat and fade

Verse 3:
Didn't take too long before I found out
What people mean by "down and out."

Spent my money, took my car,
Started telling her friends she gonna be a star.

I don't know, but I been told,
A big-legged woman ain't got no soul.
(To Chorus:)

Verse 4:
All I ask for, all I pray,
Steady-rolling woman gonna come my way.

Need a woman gonna hold my hand,
Won't tell me no lies, make me a happy man.
Ah ah ah ah ah ah ah ah ah ah ah ah ah.
(To Guitar Solo:)

D'YER MAK'ER

Note: The original recording sounds an eighth tone (25 cents) flat of concert pitch.
To play along, tune all strings slightly flat.

Words and Music by
JIMMY PAGE, JOHN BONHAM,
JOHN PAUL JONES, and ROBERT PLANT

23

Guitar Solo: (Note: This solo looks more complicated than it really is. Before trying to play it on guitar, sing the solo along with the recording to get familiar with its melodic aspects.)

DANCING DAYS

Elec. Gtr. in Open G tuning:
⑥ = D   ③ = G
⑤ = G   ② = B
④ = D   ①= D

Words and Music by
JIMMY PAGE and ROBERT PLANT

Moderate rock ♩ = 116

Intro:

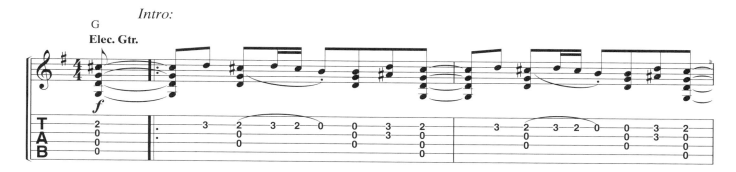

Verse 1:

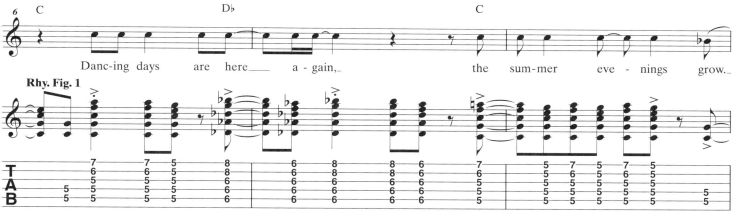

Danc-ing days are here_ a-gain,_ the sum-mer eve-nings grow._

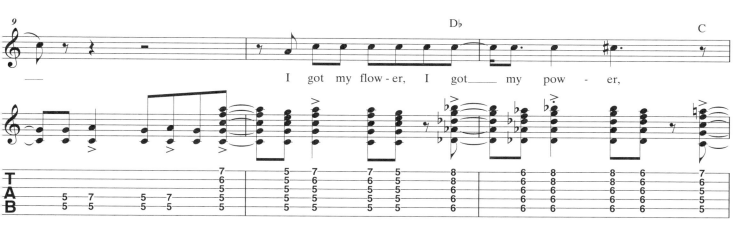

— I got my flow-er, I got_ my pow-er,

Dancing Days - 7 - 1

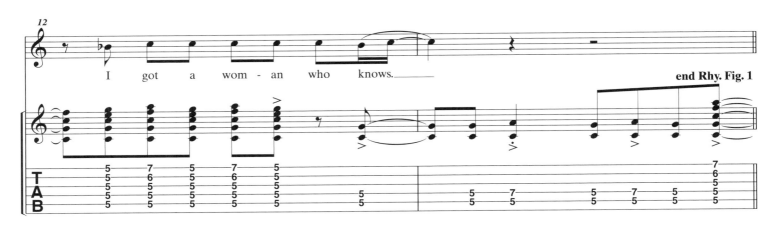

Chorus:

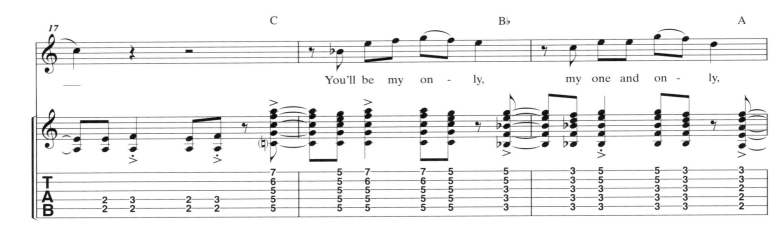

Verse 3:

Chorus:

w/Rhy. Fig. 4 *(Elec. Gtr.) see meas. 30*

I said, it's all_____ right,_____ you know it's all_____ right,_____

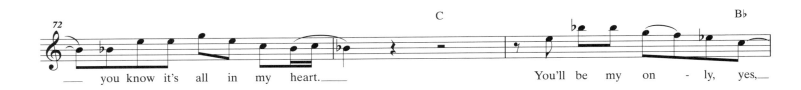

_____ you know it's all in my heart._____ You'll be my on - ly, yes,_____

_____ my one and on - ly, yes,_____ is that the way it should start?_____ I know that it's right._____

Interlude:

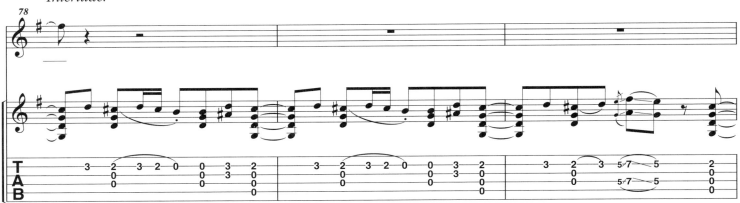

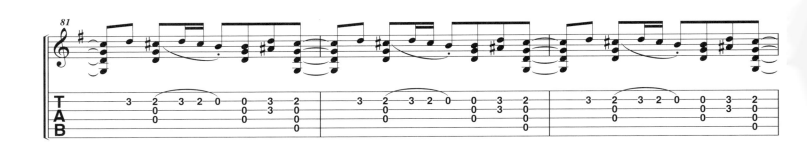

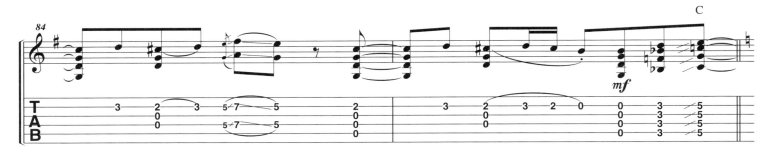

Guitar Solo:

Outro:

GOOD TIMES BAD TIMES

Moderately ♩ = 95

Intro:

Words and Music by
JIMMY PAGE, JOHN PAUL JONES
and JOHN BONHAM

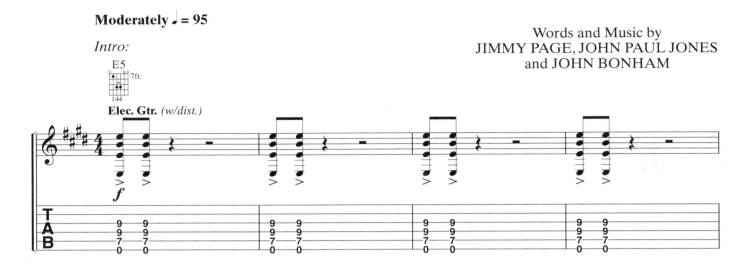

Verse 1:

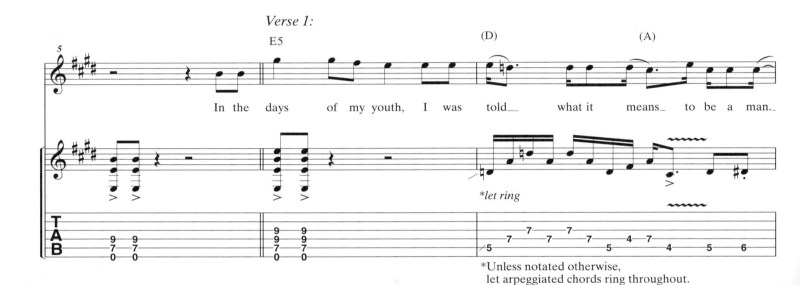

In the days of my youth, I was told ___ what it means ___ to be a man.

*let ring

*Unless notated otherwise,
let arpeggiated chords ring throughout.

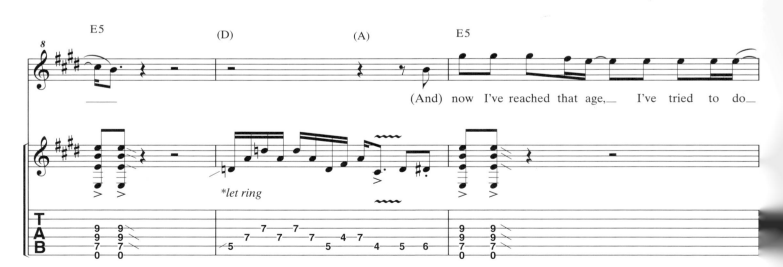

(And) now I've reached that age, ___ I've tried to do ___

*let ring

Good Times Bad Times - 5 - 1

still don't seem to care.____

Six - teen, I fell__ in love__ with a girl as sweet as could be.__ It

on - ly took a cou - ple of days__ till she was rid of me.__ She

swore that she would be__ all mine and love me till the end.__ But

Chorus:

Guitar Solo:

HOUSES OF THE HOLY

Moderately fast ♩ = 120

Intro:

Words and Music by
JIMMY PAGE and ROBERT PLANT

Verse:

1. Let me take___ you to___ the mov-ies, can I take_ ___ you to___ the show?___ Let me be___ yours ev-er tru-___ you to___
2. There's an an-gel on___ my shoul-der, in my hand, ___ a sword_ of gold.___ Let me wan-der in___ your gar-

on - ly, on - ly drive_ you mad.___ Does it hurt___ to___ hear them ly - ing?___

_ Was this the on - ly world you had?___

_ Oh.___

IMMIGRANT SONG

Moderately ♩ = 113

Words and Music by
JIMMY PAGE and ROBERT PLANT

Immigrant Song - 4 - 1

44

IN THE EVENING

Words and Music by
JOHN PAUL JONES, JIMMY PAGE
and ROBERT PLANT

Freely

*Sound effects w/bowed guitar
for approx. 50 seconds*

In the eve - ning,

Moderate rock ♩ = 104

Verse 1:

when the day is done,

Rhy. Fig. 1

I'm look-ing for a wom-an,   oh,   but the girl _____

vib. bar   P.M.

*Dip performed on recording w/vibrato bar but may be simulated with a pull off to the open string.

_____ don't come. _____   So don't let _____ her

vib. bar

In the Evening - 6 - 1

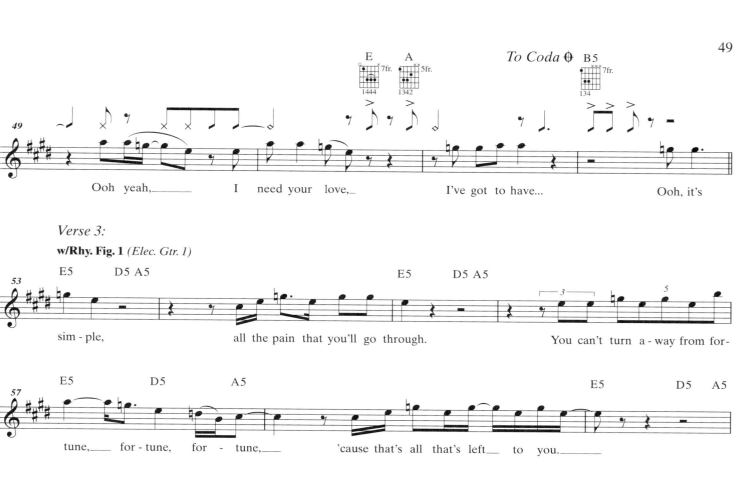

Ooh yeah,____ I need your love,__ I've got to have... Ooh, it's

Verse 3:

w/Rhy. Fig. 1 *(Elec. Gtr. 1)*

sim - ple, all the pain that you'll go through. You can't turn a - way from for-

tune,____ for - tune, for - tune,____ 'cause that's all that's left__ to you.____

Hey, it's lone-ly at the bot - tom, man,____ it's diz-zy at the

top. But when you're stand - ing in the mid-dle, oh,____

ain't no way you gon-na stop. Oh, *ba - by,*

Guitar Solo: (Note: This solo is virtuoso stuff–but we thought you might want to try it. If not, play Rhy. Fig. 1 through this section.)
w/Rhy. Fig. 1 *(Elec. Gtr. 1)* simile

Elec. Gtr. 2

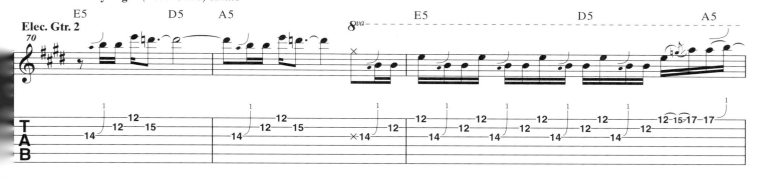

KASHMIR

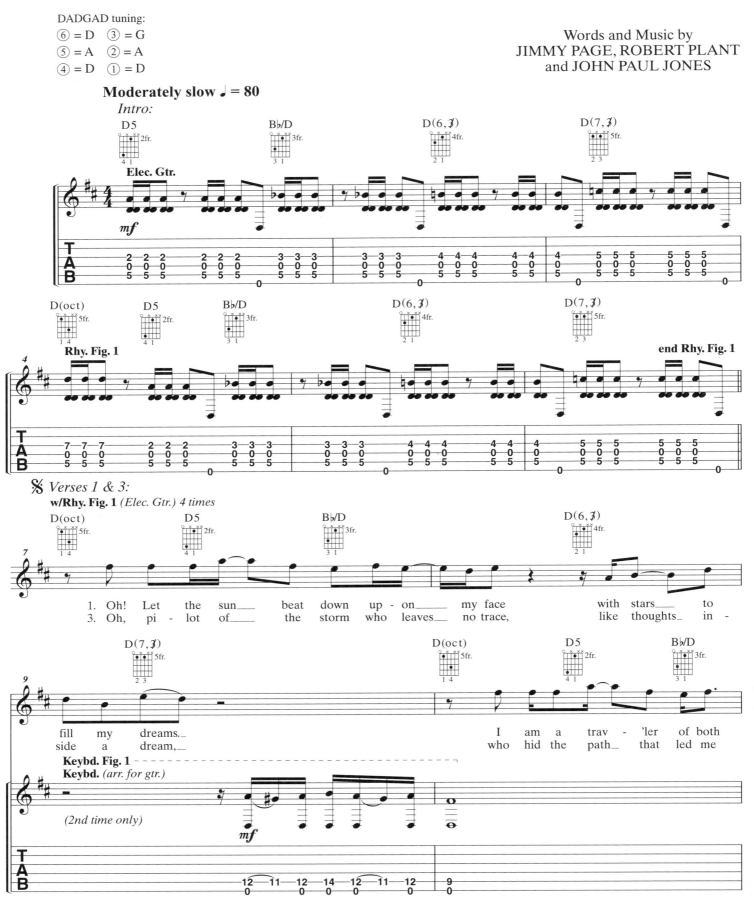

Words and Music by
JIMMY PAGE, ROBERT PLANT
and JOHN PAUL JONES

Kashmir - 7 - 1

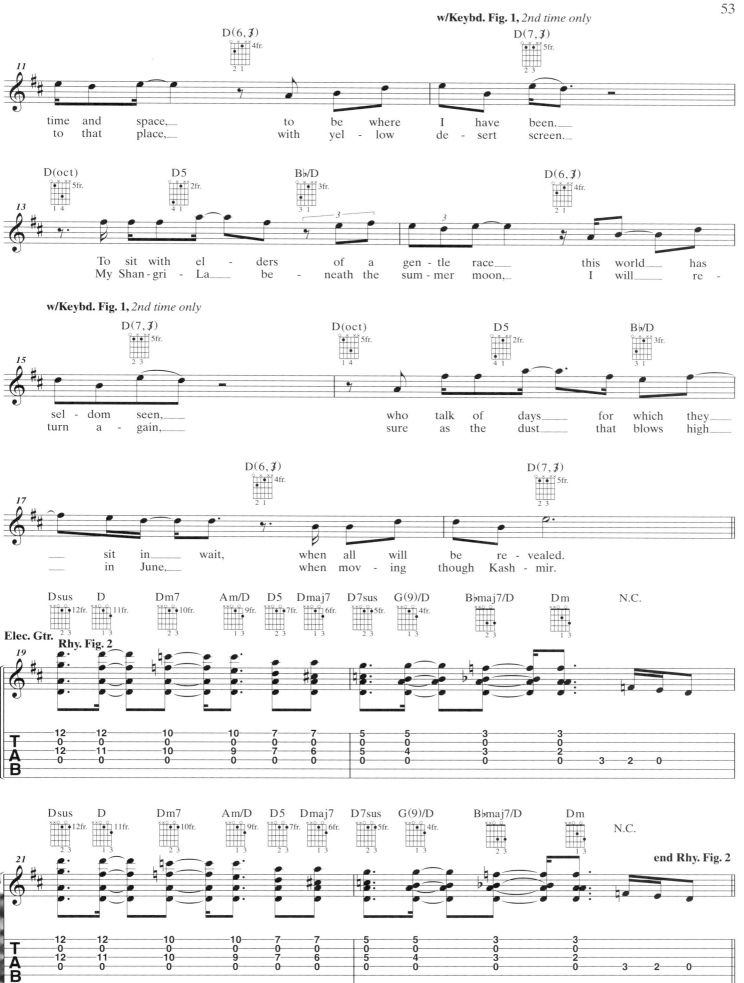

Verses 2 & 4:

w/Rhy. Fig. 1 *(Elec. Gtr.) 4 times*

2. With talk and song__ from tongues of lilt - ing grace,__ the sounds ca -
4. Oh, fa - ther of__ the four winds, fill my sails,__ to cross the

w/Keybd. Fig. 1, *both times*

ress my ear.____ Though not a word__ I heard could I__
sea of years,__ with no pro - vi - sion but an o -

w/Keybd. Fig. 1, *both times*

__ re - late, the sto - ry was quite clear.__ }
- pen face to flaunt__ the straits of fear.__ }

w/Keybd. Fig. 1, *both times*

Oh, whoa._____

Oh, whoa._____

D.S. % al Coda

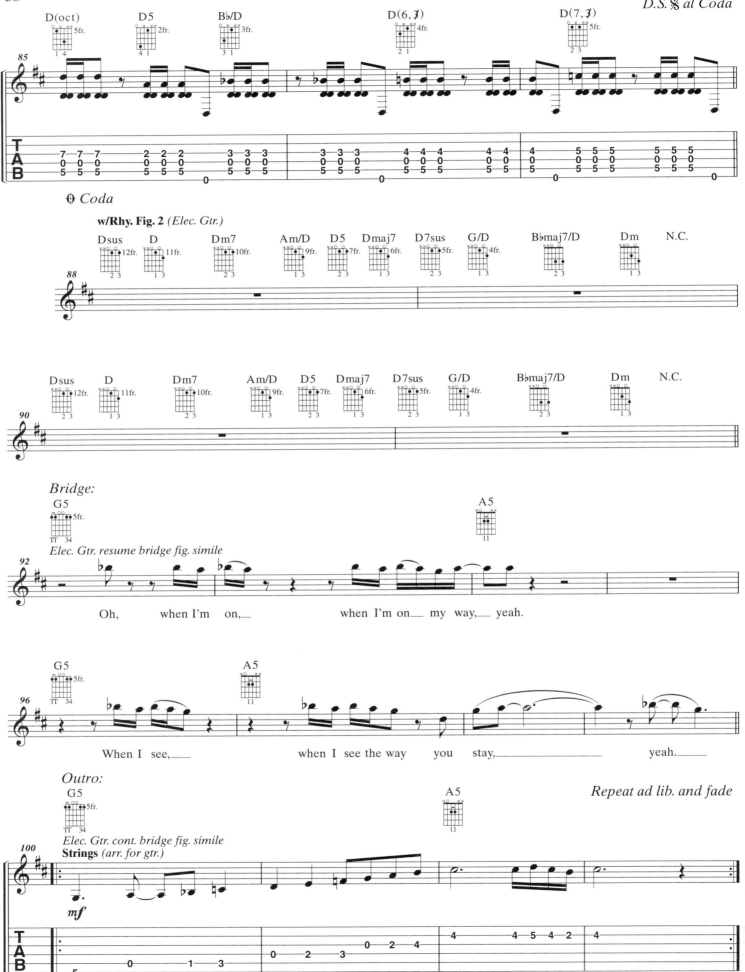

LIVING LOVING MAID
(She's Just a Woman)

Words and Music by
JIMMY PAGE and ROBERT PLANT

Fast rock ♩ = 152

Verse 1:

Living Loving Maid (She's Just a Woman) - 7 - 1

Living Loving Maid (She's Just a Woman) - 7 - 2

Living Loving Maid (She's Just a Woman) - 7 - 3

64

Living Loving Maid (She's Just a Woman) - 7 - 6

Living Loving Maid (She's Just a Woman) - 7 - 7

THE OCEAN

Moderately ♩ = 90

Words and Music by
JOHN BONHAM, JOHN PAUL JONES,
JIMMY PAGE and ROBERT PLANT

The Ocean - 10 - 2

Verse 2:

Sing - ing to an o - cean, I can hear the o - cean's roar.

Bkgrd. Vcls.: Ooh.____

Rhy. Fig. 2

end Rhy. Fig. 2

w/Rhy. Fig. 2 *(Elec. Gtr. 1) 2 times (see meas. 22–23)*

Play for__ free, play__ for me,__ play a whole lot more,__ more.__

Ooh.__

Sing-ing'bout the good_things, _____ and the sun that lights__ the day.____

Ooh.____

I used to sing to the moun - tains, has the o - cean lost__ its__ way?

Elec. Gtr. 1

Guitar Solo: (Note: This solo and the Outro beginning in measure 70 are optional.
You may play the Rhy. Fig. if the solo is too difficult.)

w/Rhy. Fig. 1 *(Elec. Gtr. 1) 2 times (see meas. 1–4)*

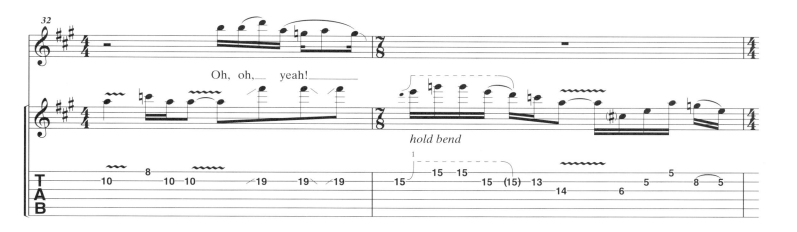

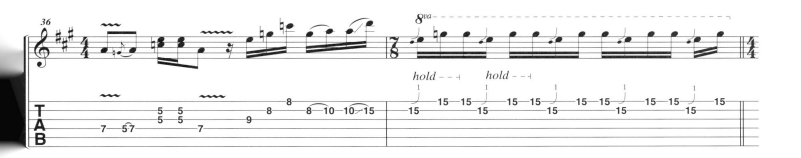

The Ocean - 10 - 4

*Chord suffixes in parenthesis indicate composite harmony.

Verse 3: *(band enters)*
w/Rhy. Fig. 2 *(Elec. Gtr. 1) 3 times (see meas. 22–23)*

Sit - ting 'round_____ sing - ing songs_ till the night_ turns in - to day._____

Bkgrd. Vcls.: Ooh.____

Used to sing a - bout moun - tains, but the moun - tains washed_ a - way.___

Ooh.____

Now I'm sing - ing all__ my songs_ to the girl_ who won my heart._

Ooh.____

She is on - ly three_ years old,_ and it's a real fine way to start._____

Elec. Gtr. 1

72

ROCK AND ROLL

Words and Music by
JIMMY PAGE, ROBERT PLANT,
JOHN PAUL JONES and JOHN BONHAM

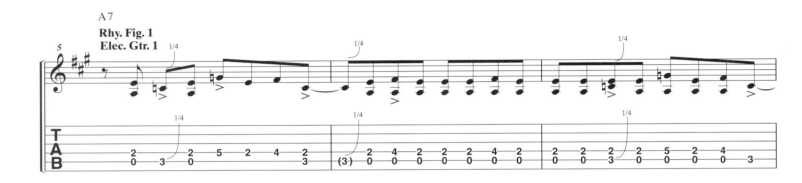

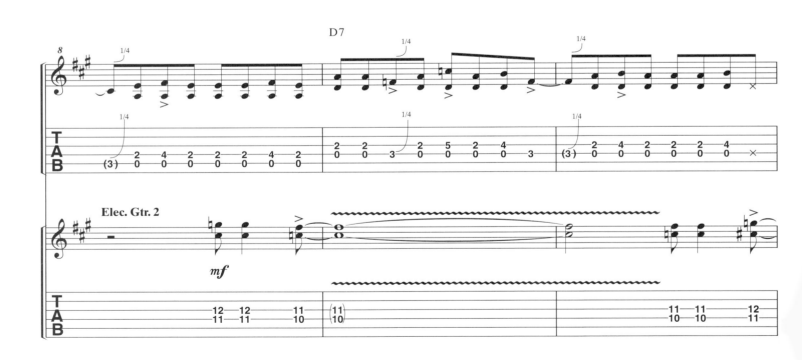

Rock and Roll - 10 - 1

D Interlude:

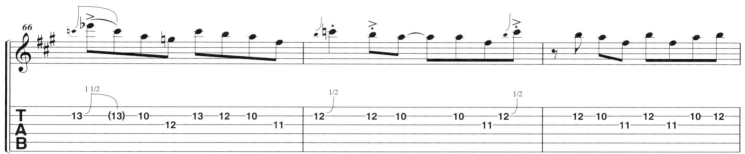

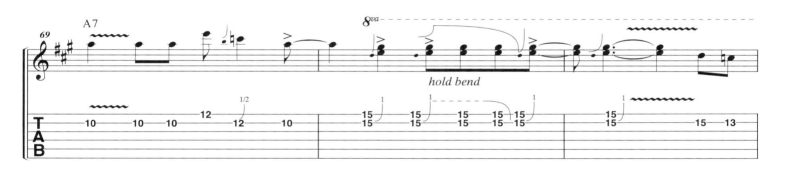

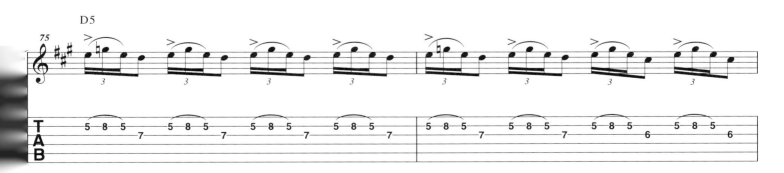

Rock and Roll - 10 - 6

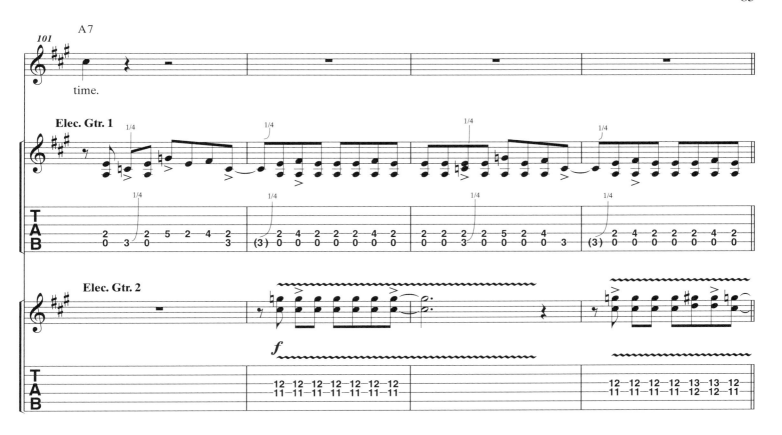

G Outro:

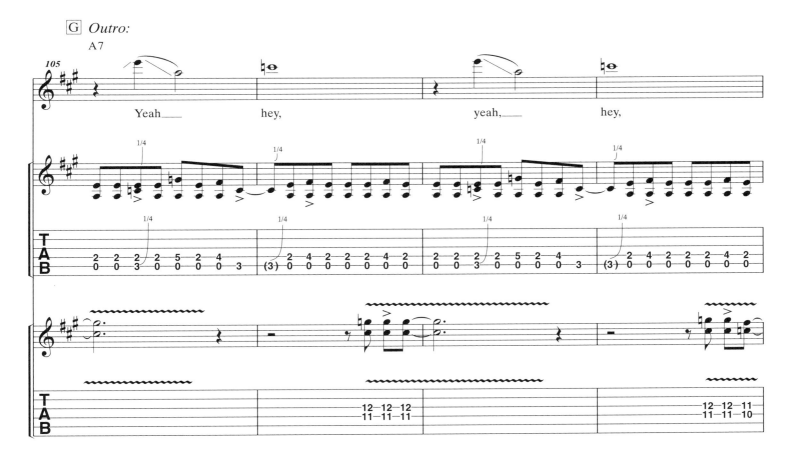

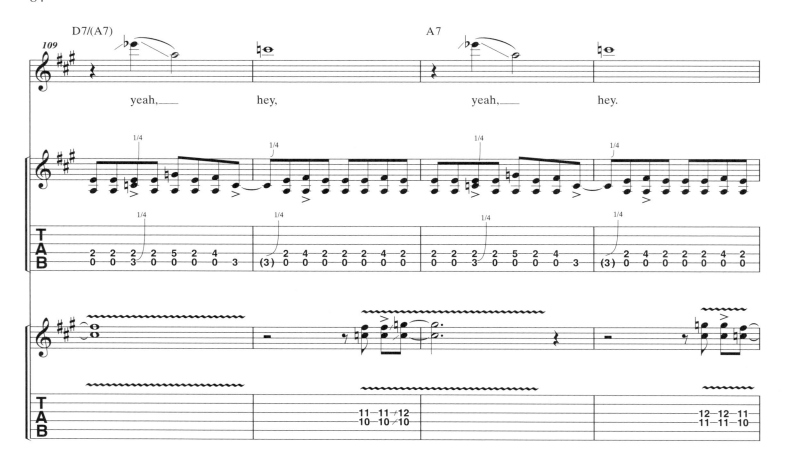

yeah,_____   hey,   yeah,_____   hey.

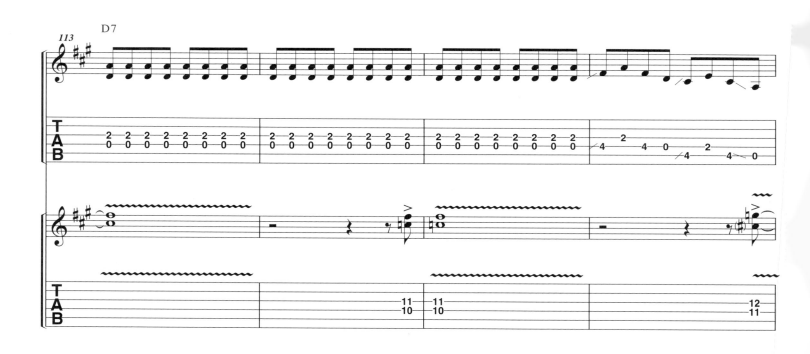

OVER THE HILLS AND FAR AWAY

Words and Music by
JIMMY PAGE and ROBERT PLANT

Moderate rock ♩ = 98

Intro:

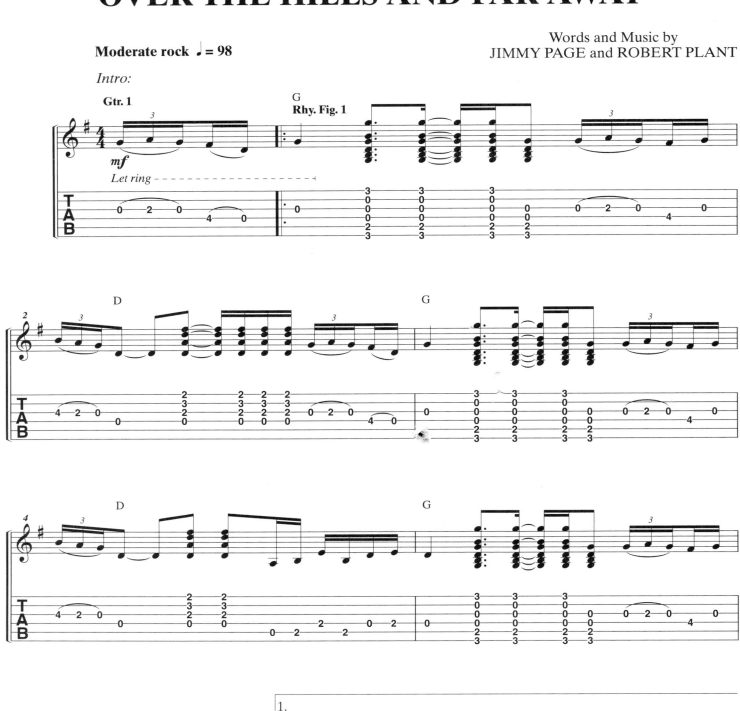

Over the Hills and Far Away - 9 - 1

88

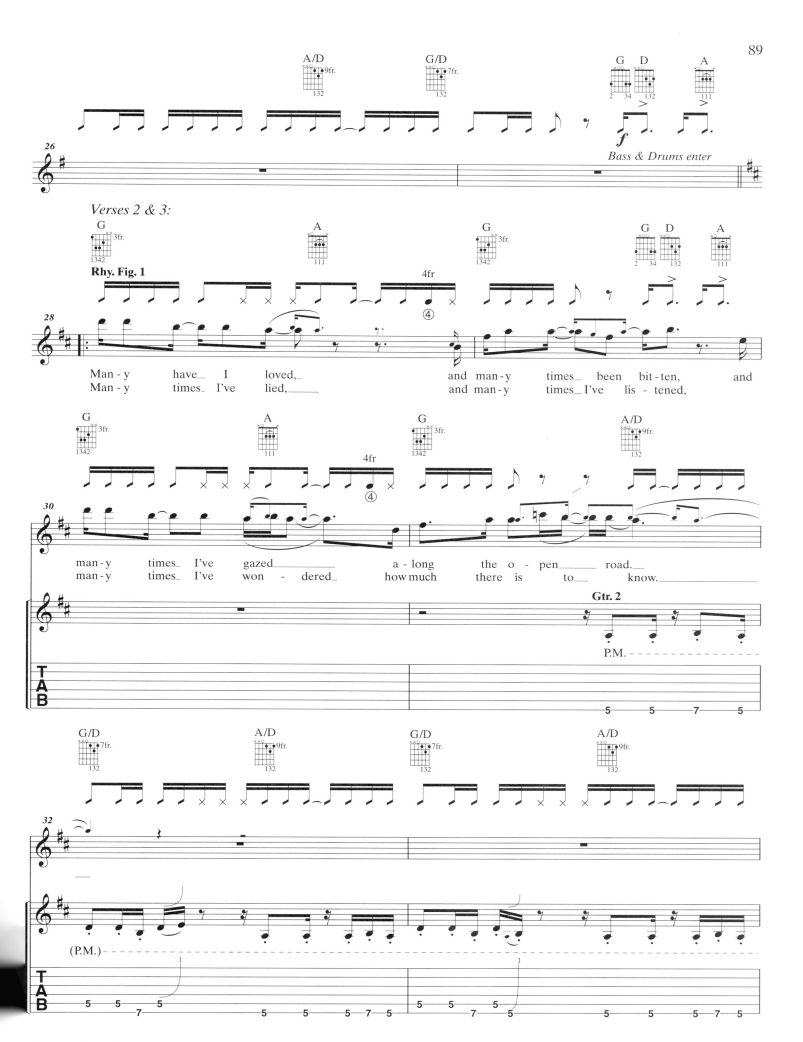

Verse 4:

w/Rhy. Fig. 1 *(Gtr. 1) see meas. 28–35*

Man - y dreams__ come true, and some have sil - ver lin - ings. I__

__ live for my dream,__ and a pock - et - ful of__ gold._____

Gtr. 1

Gtr. 2 *(Gtr. 1 cont. simile)*

Guitar Solo: (Note: The guitar solo by Gtr. 2 is optional. Feel free to keep playing Rhy. Fig. 2.)

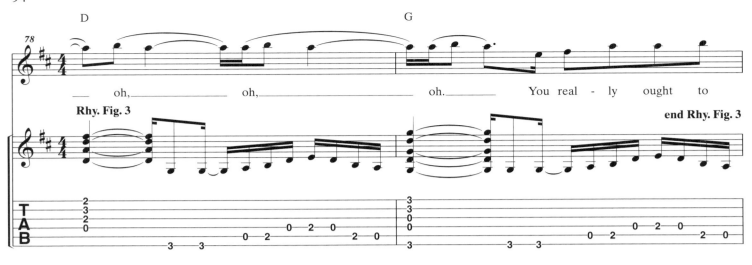

oh,_____ oh,_____ oh._____ You real - ly ought to

Rhy. Fig. 3

end Rhy. Fig. 3

w/Rhy. Fig. 3 *(Gtr.1)* till fade out

Start fade

know,_____ oh,_____ oh._____ I real - ly ought to know._____

Keyboards enter

Oh,_____ you know_ I_____ should, you know_ I should, you know_

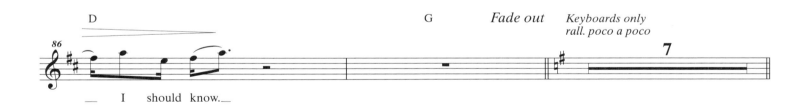

Fade out Keyboards only
rall. poco a poco

_ I should know._

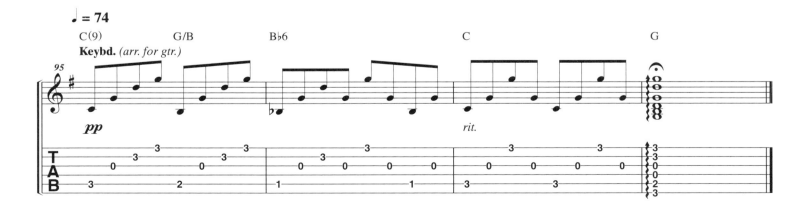

♩ = 74

Keybd. *(arr. for gtr.)*

pp

rit.

STAIRWAY TO HEAVEN

Words and Music by
JIMMY PAGE and ROBERT PLANT

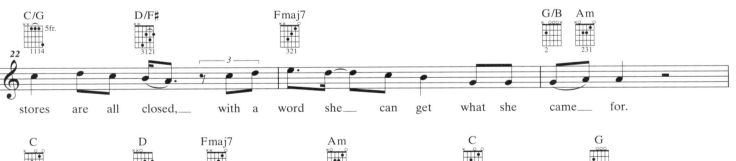

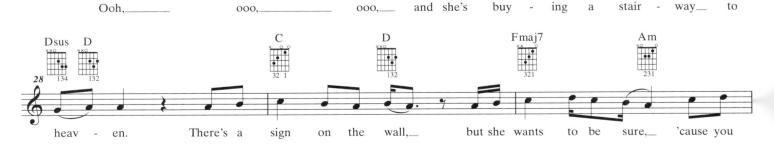

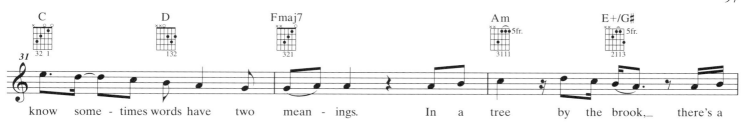

know some-times words have two mean-ings. In a tree by the brook,__ there's a

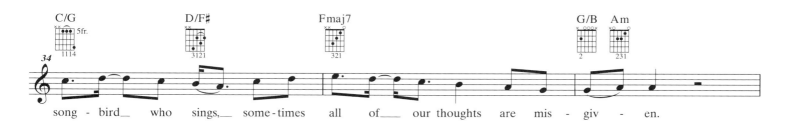

song-bird__ who sings,__ some-times all of__ our thoughts are mis-giv-en.

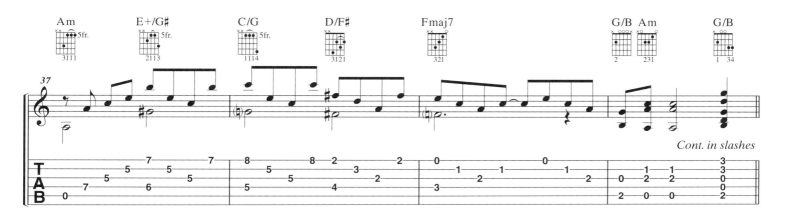

Cont. in slashes

Interlude:

Rhy. Fig. 1

Ooh,_____ it makes we won-der.

end Rhy. Fig. 1

Ooh,_____ it makes me won-der._____ 2. There's a

Verses 2 & 3: ♩ = **83**

100

Bridge: ♩ = **102**

And as we wind__ on down the road,__

our shad-ows tall - er than our soul._____ There walks a la - dy we all

know,_____ who shines white light and wants to

show,___ how ev - 'ry - thing__ still turns to gold.____

And if you lis - ten ver - y hard,_____ the tune will come to you__ at

last.___ When all are one__ and one is all,_____

WHOLE LOTTA LOVE

Words and Music by
JIMMY PAGE, ROBERT PLANT,
JOHN PAUL JONES, JOHN BONHAM
and WILLIE DIXON

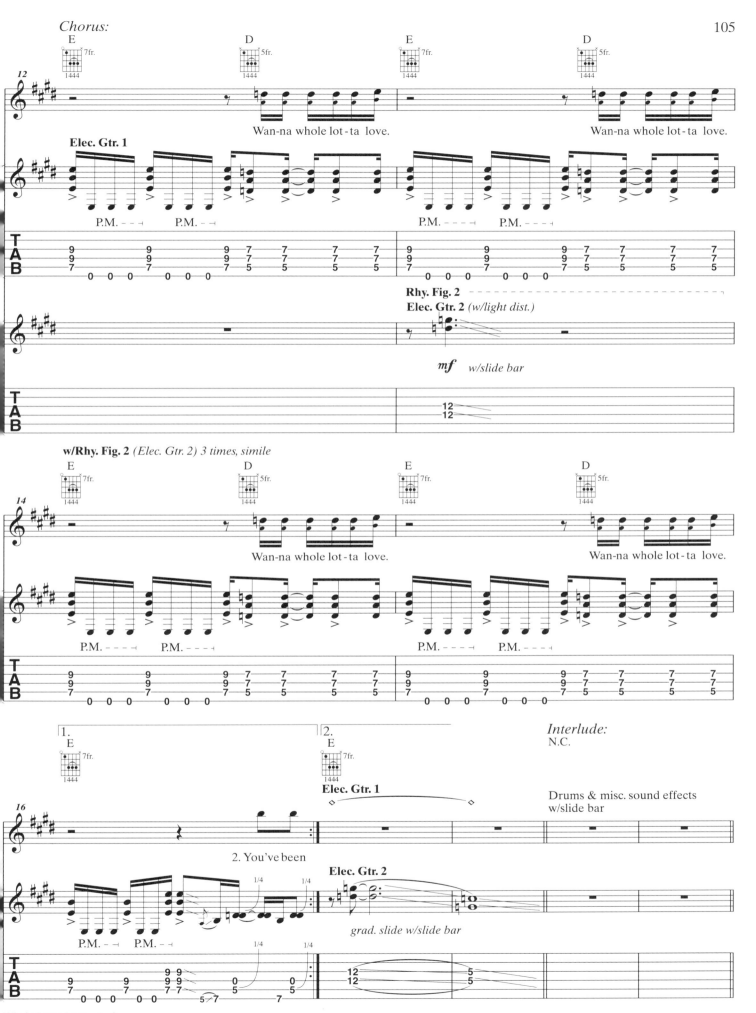

Whole Lotta Love - 4 - 2

Guitar Solo: (Note: This solo has some rapid-fire licks. If they're a little too fast right now, start slow and build up your speed.)

Verse 2:
You've been learning, and, baby, I been learning.
All them good times, baby, baby, I've been yearning.
Way, way down inside, honey, you need.
I'm gonna give you my love.
I'm gonna give you my love.
(To Chorus:)

Verse 3:
You've been cooling, and, baby, I've been drooling.
All the good times, baby, I've been misusing.
Way, way down inside, I'm gonna give you my love.
I'm gonna give you every inch of my love.
I'm gonna give you my love.
(To Chorus:)

GUITAR TAB GLOSSARY

TABLATURE EXPLANATION

TAB illustrates the six strings of the guitar.
Notes and chords are indicated by the placement of fret numbers.

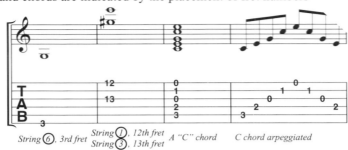

String ⑥, 3rd fret   *String ①, 12th fret*   *A "C" chord*   *C chord arpeggiated*
                        String ③, 13th fret

BENDING NOTES

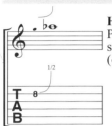

Half Step:
Play the note and bend string one half step (one fret).

Whole Step:
Play the note and bend string one whole step (two frets).

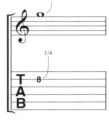

Slight Bend/ Quarter-Tone Bend:
Play the note and bend string sharp.

Prebend and Release:
Play the already-bent string, then immediately drop it down to the fretted note.

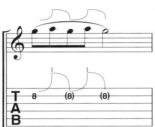

Bend and Release:
Play the note and bend to the next pitch, then release to the original note. Only the first note is attacked.

PICK DIRECTION

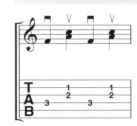

Downstrokes and Upstrokes:
The downstroke is indicated with this symbol (⊓) and the upstroke is indicated with this (∨).

ARTICULATIONS

Hammer On:
Play the lower note, then "hammer" your finger to the higher note. Only the first note is plucked.

Pull Off:
Play the higher note with your first finger already in position on the lower note. Pull your finger off the first note with a strong downward motion that plucks the string—sounding the lower note.

Palm Mute:
The notes are muted (muffled) by placing the palm of the pick hand lightly on the strings, just in front of the bridge.

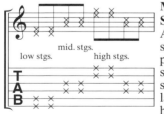

Muted Strings:
A percussive sound is produced by striking the strings while laying the fret hand across them.

Legato Slide:
Play the first note and, keeping pressure applied on the string, slide up to the second note. The diagonal line shows that it is a slide and not a hammer-on or a pull-off.

HARMONICS

Natural Harmonic:
A finger of the fret hand lightly touches the string at the note indicated in the TAB and is plucked by the pick producing a bell-like sound called a harmonic.

RHYTHM SLASHES

Strum Marks/ Rhythm Slashes:
Strum with the indicated rhythm pattern. Strum marks can be located above the staff or within the staff.

Single Notes with Rhythm Slashes:
Sometimes single notes are incorporated into a strum pattern. The circled number below is the string and the fret number is above.

Artificial Harmonic:
Fret the note at the first TAB number, lightly touch the string at the fret indicated in parens (usually 12 frets higher than the fretted note), then pluck the string with an available finger or your pick.